Living the Days of Lent 2007

Edited by
Sister Anita M. Constance, SC

Paulist Press
New York / Mahwah, N.J.

Illustrated by Eileen Herb-Witte

ISBN: 0-8091-4390-9

Published by Paulist Press
997 Macarthur Boulevard
Mahwah, New Jersey 07430

www.paulistpress.com

Printed and bound in the
United States of America

Thurs

Thursday, February 22: Feast of the Chair of Peter

GRACE IN WEAKNESS

When Jesus asked his disciples, "Who do you say I am?" only Peter responded, and none of the others contradicted him or objected to this profession of faith.

Peter—quick to respond, often to blunder, and always to repent. This time his impetuosity was approved and blessed with the greatest honor and awesome responsibility: Peter became the shepherd. Not that he was *above* the others, but a shepherd who was also a member of the flock. In the end, he would join the others, handing himself over to Jesus for all eternity.

Like Peter, our weakness can become our grace. With our eyes on Jesus and our hearts on what is good, just, and loving, we, too, will be able to hand ourselves over to the Shepherd of our heart for all eternity.

"He leads me in right paths for his name's sake. Even though I walk through the darkest valley, I fear no evil; for you are with me; your rod and your staff—they comfort me" (Ps 23:3–4).

READINGS:
1 Peter 5:1–4; Psalm 23; Matthew 16:13–19

Fr⟶

Friday, February 23

POVERTY OF LIMITATION

As much as we might want to, most of us cannot actually give bread to the hungry, or clothe the naked, or shelter the homeless the way we would like. So we *fast*—denying ourselves food and pleasures—hoping to experience, in the only way we can, what it means to be poor.

But will we ever really *know*? What is it like to have to ask another for our needs; to be without basic human rights; to wait for someone else to make decisions that affect our lives? To be poor is to have a hunger that can only be satisfied by a just society.

Perhaps holding our tongue this Lent, when we would like to speak, will remind us of those voiceless ones who are allowed no choices, whose cry is from the silent depths where they seek a way to step into what is rightly theirs.

"The sacrifice acceptable to God is a broken spirit…" (Ps 51:17).
Enable us, O God, to help our brothers and sisters in some small way to satisfy their hunger this Lent.

READINGS:
Isaiah 58:1–9; Psalm 51; Matthew 9:14–15

Sat

Saturday, February 24

GOD'S SIMPLICITY

We learn from experience early in life that if you touch a hot stove, then you will get burned. If you walk out in the rain, then you will get wet. If you jump into the air, then you will return to the ground.

God's law is simple, and equally as certain and unchanging as the law of gravity. Yet God is not an immutable judge of our foibles and weaknesses. Experience should tell us that, as we come to greater knowledge of God through the deepening of our relationship over the years.

If God's law teaches us anything, it teaches us the importance of *unconditional love,* a love that is both challenging but still forgiving. During Lent, let us reflect on this law and the possibility of meeting its challenge, as well as receiving the embrace that God offers.

"Teach me your way, O LORD, that I may walk in your truth" (Ps 86:11). *Help me to trust in your goodness as I strive to be good.*

READINGS:
Isaiah 58:9–14; Psalm 86; Luke 5:27–32

First Sunday of Lent, February 25

THE DIVINE INDWELLING

Jesus was like us in all things, therefore he had to struggle with the same temptations we do. But the scriptures add "except sin." Unfortunately, those few words have become an excuse for many to give up, or to claim humanness as weakness. After all, Jesus "made it" because he was God.

I think Jesus "made it" because he knew who he was: a dwelling place of God. This knowledge had deepened over a lifetime so that when temptation came, he just couldn't give in. How could he allow any of his actions to defile the temple of God?

We are the dwelling place of God, as well. We know that, but do we realize the precious treasure we carry? Do we honor this temple of divinity that we are? Can we at least begin to get a glimpse of ourselves as the earthen vessel God has chosen to live within?

Perhaps this Lent is the time to begin remembering God's word: "Because you have made the LORD your refuge, the Most High your dwelling place, no evil shall befall you…" (Ps 91:9–10).

READINGS:
Deuteronomy 26:4–10; Psalm 91; Romans 10:8–13; Luke 4:1–13

Monday, February 26

THE BLESSING OF THE LEAST

The Book of Leviticus is often referred to as the "Law of Holiness." God's compassionate mandate is clear: "You shall love your neighbor as yourself" (Lev 19:18). This profound Old Testament directive is brought to fulfillment in the New Covenant as Jesus tells us that he is our neighbor. Jesus is the person who lives with us, works with us, prays with us. Jesus is the poor among us, the needy, the fearful.

His invitation is upon us: "Truly I tell you; just as you did it to one of the least of these who are members of my family you did it to me" (Matt 25:40).

Yes…"the decrees of the LORD are sure, making wise the simple" (Ps 19:7). *Lord, may the inward journey of Lent bring us wisdom enough to truly recognize and love you in all we meet this day.*

READINGS:
Leviticus 19:1–2, 11–18; Psalm 19; Matthew 25:31–46

Tuesday, February 27

WORD OF GOD

As rain saturates and renews parched earth—

so God's Word: softens the landscape of our heart
fills in the contours of the soul
soaks into the fiber of each life
drenches our day with grace.

God's Word invites us into Divine Mystery—
teaching us: to pray
to love
to forgive.

God's Word is—
clear and insistent: as we forgive, so we shall be forgiven.

"The LORD is near…" (Ps 34:18). *As the days of Lent unfold, may God's word bear fruit in our lives.*

READINGS:
Isaiah 55:10–11; Psalm 34; Matthew 6:7–15

Introduction

The heart of the gospel is *forgiveness.* It is key to Jesus' mission of boundless love. Forgiveness precedes many of his healings. It is the heart of so many of his parables. It became—and still is—the steppingstone to love because forgiveness frees us to love.

We have been forgiven; we *all* have. How has this changed our lives? How has this increased our love? How has this changed the lives of those with whom we live and work? This Lent, our awareness, our perspective, our works of charity will be influenced by the fruitful reflection on God's forgiveness of us. The truth that sets us free will begin a chain reaction that can change our world!

—Anita M. Constance, SC
Editor

wed

Ash Wednesday, February 21

CHANGES IN THE AIR

Lent is *not* a quiet time. There is a rumble of discontent in the air. The readings begin with the sound of trumpets summoning all the people to listen, to become stirred up, to move beyond.

For the long-awaited Savior is preparing to fulfill his mission, aware of what lies ahead—the awesome and terrible encounter with the forces of evil—a battle for the conquest of the soul.

The trumpet sounds for us, too, demanding that we cry out for mercy, with indignation for the crimes committed against the powerless, for courage to cast away from us whatever would hold us back from following Jesus. The enemies we have to overcome are deep within us—desires for power, prestige, pleasure, self-will—all quite subtle at times, but still there.

"O Lord, open my lips, and my mouth will declare your praise" (Ps 51:15), *and I will thank you and bless you forever.*

READINGS:
Joel 2:12–18; Psalm 51; 2 Corinthians 5:20—6:2;
Matthew 6:1–6, 16–18

Wednesday, February 28

MAGNETIC MYSTERY

The biblical allegory of Jonah is rich in
    the message of hope and
    the challenge of repentance.

    Daily, God is calling us to respond in faith. Like Jonah, at times we resist the mystery of God's call. But such mystery is stronger and more magnetic than our every effort to ignore it. Salvation history brims over with
    the depth of God's merciful love,
    the certainty of God's fidelity and
    the generosity of God's unconditional forgiveness.

    These assurances are ours, as we tend to God's promptings each day.

O God, "Restore in me the joy of your salvation and sustain in me a willing spirit" (Ps 51:12). Lord, may we remain open to the mystery of your call and be willing to follow where you lead us.

READINGS:
Jonah 3:1–10; Psalm 51; Luke 11:29–32

Thursday, March 1

COURAGE TO TRUST

Jesus urges and encourages us to approach God in complete trust and utter confidence: *"How much more will your Father in heaven give good things to those who ask"* (Matt 7:11).

Our every need for soul-growth is intimately hinged to the powerful truth of God's faithful generosity. Lent provides us with an opportunity to ask, seek, and find—

to ask for deeper insight into the complex questions of our times,

to seek freedom from the false notion of solitary salvation,

to find the deep peace which only our loving God can give.

"On the day I called, you answered me; you increased my strength of soul" (Ps 138:3). *Gracious God, wake us up that we may more fully accept your continuous love and guidance.*

READINGS:
Esther C:12, 14–16, 23–25; Psalm 138; Matthew 7:7–12

Friday, March 2

HEALING FORGIVENESS

Often the first step to reconciliation is facing the truth within ourselves—our own need to have a forgiving heart. We hear the Lenten call to examine our relationships and mend those torn by anger, jealousy, misunderstanding, or fear. How can we approach the altar of God without taking this first step? Humility and courage are the pathways to the purity of heart that we seek. Can we walk along this road? Yes, because Jesus leads the way; he asks only that we follow. Let us enter into our hearts today, keeping our eyes on Jesus, and ask him to carve out the truth we seek.

God of all kindness, we know that "with [you] there is steadfast love, and the power to redeem" (Ps 130:7). Hear us this Lent and help us to open ourselves to these and all your saving gifts.

READINGS:
Ezekiel 18:21–28; Psalm 130; Matthew 5:20–26

Saturday, March 3

ACCEPTING DIFFERENCES

"Love your enemies and pray for those who persecute you."
—Matthew 5:44

In this war-ravaged world, these words bring us up short, for they are the essential call of Jesus.

Who are our enemies? The international scene is a confusion of wars, hostile acts, and misunderstandings. Yet the people of these nations are our sisters and brothers in the human family. What are our differences? Do they really have to become the challenge that sets us one against the other?

At home, are those who think differently, live and pray differently than we—are *they* the enemy? There will never be peace unless nations and peoples look beyond the differences we perceive in each other. There will never be peace in our lives unless we respect our differences and walk the bridge of reconciliation.

Creator of us all, "with my whole heart I seek you" (Ps 119:10), and beg for the strength for us to believe in one another and to trust that this will make a difference.

READINGS:
Deuteronomy 26:16–19; Psalm 119; Matthew 5:43–48

Second Sunday of Lent, March 4

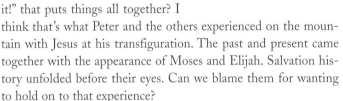

REMEMBERING

Did you ever have one of those "aha!" moments? That inner "I get it!" that puts things all together? I think that's what Peter and the others experienced on the mountain with Jesus at his transfiguration. The past and present came together with the appearance of Moses and Elijah. Salvation history unfolded before their eyes. Can we blame them for wanting to hold on to that experience?

So often, though, keeping something as close and vibrant to us as it was at the moment of discovery is not possible. We, too, have to come down the mountain and walk along the plainness of everyday life. Yet part of us never really forgets the feeling and the surprise. I don't think the disciples ever forgot.

Maybe during Lent we could linger with those moments a bit. Savor again the joy, freedom, and encouragement they brought us. Despite the disappointment the disciples experienced when it was over, they *still* had Jesus. We, too, still have Jesus as we pray:

"The LORD is my light and my salvation…The LORD is the stronghold of my life; of whom shall I be afraid?" (Ps 27:1).

READINGS:
Genesis 15:5–12, 17–18; Psalm 119; Philippians 3:17—4:1;
Luke 9:28–36

Monday, March 5

THE COST OF JUDGING

The biblical call to mercy and forgiveness is often deafened by our limited understanding and narrowness of heart. It is not difficult to criticize or judge another, when we base our opinion upon our own experiences and beliefs. Frequently, we are unaware of the burden others carry or the difficulties they are attempting to cope with.

The Lenten call to repentance and forgiveness compels us not only to examine ourselves about how we have failed, but also to give greater effort to understanding and accepting all those we meet, *without* the price of judgment, for this is a costly burden for anyone to bear.

"Help us, O God of our salvation, for the glory of your name; deliver us and forgive our sins for your name's sake" (Ps 79:9). *Strengthen our efforts to be nonjudgmental, accepting, and forgiving this season and always.*

READINGS:
Daniel 9:4–10; Psalm 79; Luke 6:36–38

Tuesday, March 6

SETTING FREE

Isaiah's admonition to "wash ourselves clean" and seek justice urges us to reflect upon the injustice in the world around us, as well as the international scene. Such reflection compels us to action on behalf of those who cannot speak for themselves.

Often the scope of injustice can overwhelm us and promote inertia and the sin of sloth. As responsible Christians, we must seek ways to help those burdened by the oppression of poverty, disease, lack of education, and other societal ills.

As we try to help the disadvantaged in our world, we must also uncover the reasons for their plight and use our collective voice to urge systemic change. Yes, the needs are overwhelming, but each one of us has a voice.

All-just One, "Out of Zion, the perfection of beauty, God shines forth" (Ps 50:2), *help us this day to be beacons of justice, hope, and truth.*

READINGS:
Isaiah 1:10, 16–20; Psalm 50; Matthew 23:1–12

Wednesday, March 7

THE PRESENCE OF GOD

"You do not know what you are asking. Are you able to drink the cup that I am about to drink?"
—Matthew 20:22

In the quote above Jesus is referring to his suffering, passion, and death. How many of us would have the confidence to respond as John and James did, that we too are able? We have only to think of today's military going to war knowing their chances of returning safely are nebulous at best. They too pledge: "We are able."

I believe that John and James felt in their hearts that they could live through anything as long as Jesus was by their side. Our future is often uncertain in the best of times. But we can face each day well, just one day at a time, trusting in the loving companionship of God.

"Into your hand I commit my spirit; you have redeemed me, O LORD, faithful God" (Ps 31:5).

READINGS:
Jeremiah 18:18–20; Psalm 31; Matthew 20:17–28

Thursday, March 8

POOR IN SPIRIT

Many years ago, I had an experience that has never left me. I was attending a funeral. The church was full of women and men religious awaiting the start of the procession. Two buses arrived and more people entered the church. They were coming from a shelter in a nearby city where the deceased person had ministered to the poor for several years. There were no empty pews, so all the new arrivals lined the walls of the side aisles. It was a humbling sight for all of us.

There were many priests concelebrating; they were sitting on chairs in the sanctuary waiting for the liturgy to begin. Then, one by one, the priests motioned to the people standing in the side aisles, and directed them to the chairs in the sanctuary. The priests then took their places in the aisles. This was truly a demonstration of welcoming home the poor among us!

...their delight is in the law of the LORD, and on his law they meditate day and night (Ps 1:2).

READINGS:
Jeremiah 17:5–10; Psalm 1; Luke 16:19–31

Friday, March 9

DIVINE INSPIRATION

They said to one another, "Here comes this dreamer."

—Genesis 37:19

Can you imagine what our world would be like without dreamers? The dictionary defines a dreamer as "one who gives free reign to the imagination, a visionary." It is also a person who has the ability to understand and appreciate the creations of others, especially works of art and literature.

How dull our lives would be without music, paintings, literature! I thank God every day for the "dreamers" who give us their interpretation of the world in which we live.

O give thanks to the LORD, call on his name, make known his deeds among the peoples (Ps 105:1).

READINGS:
Genesis 37:3–4, 12–13, 17–28; Psalm 105;
Matthew 21:33–43, 45–46

Saturday, March 10

UNDERSTANDING

Today's readings blend into one, showing the forgiveness and love of God in all of creation. This invites me to reflect on how true I am to the scriptures, to live in union with the God of my creation.

Some days I find it rather difficult to ignore or overlook the thoughtlessness of others, especially when it affects my plans or activities. It now strikes me as selfish, perhaps lacking consideration of actions that I do not fully understand.

Was the person burdened with more difficulties than I could ever imagine or have experienced? Was such thoughtlessness intentional?

May this Lent give us all an opportunity to concentrate on the goodness of Jesus as he prepared himself for (and invites his loved ones to share in) the ultimate sacrifice of life—a dying to self so that others may live.

The LORD is merciful and gracious, slow to anger and abounding in steadfast love (Ps 103:8).

READINGS:
Micah 7:14–15, 18–20; Psalm 103; Luke 15:1–3, 11–32

Third Sunday of Lent, March 11

HARDNESS OF HEART

Ezekiel was sent to a people who were closed to the word he would bring them. Moses led the Israelites in the desert despite their continual return to idols. But the parable of the barren fig tree speaks of hope amid despair. At the urging of the gardener, the owner does not cut it down, but rather fertilizes and prods it to bear fruit.

Each of us has times when we close our hearts and minds to God's word. We deal with others who are unwilling to listen to us. The gospel urges us not to write others off as we might easily do, but to choose the path to life. How might we dig around the barren fig trees in our life? What might we put in the soil to promote growth and fruitfulness?

"Bless the LORD, O my soul, and all that is within me" (Ps 103:1). *We bless you, Lord, and thank you for the many times that you do not give up on us. May my ways reflect your ways and promote life in others.*

READINGS:
Exodus 3:1–8,13–15; Psalm 103; 1 Corinthians 10:1–6, 10–12; Luke 13:1–9

Monday, March 12

EXPECT THE UNEXPECTED

We are often captured by the drama of this story: mighty Naaman marching to Israel, seeking Elisha, but interacting through messengers, then washing in the Jordan to be healed of leprosy. Underneath the drama, though, are key characters: Elisha's messenger, the servant girl who suggests the possibility of healing, and Naaman's servants who convince him to wash in the river. All seem insignificant, yet are powerful in bringing God's healing to Naaman.

Naaman expected the prophet to speak to him face to face and then to heal him. But he was healed in the simple act of washing in an ordinary river. We sometimes look and listen for God in conventional places, people, and events. In our struggles we, too, need others to lead us to the healing hand of God. The messengers and the healing can come in ways that we might not expect.

"O send out your light and your truth; let them lead me" (Ps 43:3). *Open my eyes and ears to hear your word and see your face in the ordinary, the simple, the lowly, and the poor today.*

READINGS:
2 Kings 5:1–15; Psalm 42, 43; Luke 4:24–30

Tuesday, March 13

MOVING ON

"[Peter said], '...how often should
I forgive? As many as seven times?'
Jesus said to him, 'Not seven times,
but, I tell you, seventy-seven times.'"
—Matthew 18:21–22

The news told of a woman who was severely injured as the result of a teenage prank. Every bone in her face was broken in the accident. She miraculously survived and endured months of reconstructive surgery. Her perpetrator was arrested and jailed. During the trial the woman met her assailant who, in turn, expressed regret for the shortsighted prank. She later pleaded for a light sentence for him, reasoning that, grateful for her recovery, she also wanted the youth to have a second chance at life.

This was a powerful example of forgiveness that models the generosity of God and changed two lives! Perhaps the young man will gift another with forgiveness who, in turn, will forgive. Imagine a world in which we forgave each other, one person at a time. In no time the ripple effect would spread to seventy-seven times!

"Do not remember the sins of my youth..." (Ps 25:7). *And may I not remember the sins of others: sins of youth or sins of adulthood. Help me, Lord, to forgive from my heart and to love generously.*

READINGS:
Daniel 3:25, 34–43; Psalm 25; Matthew 18:21–35

Wednesday, March 14

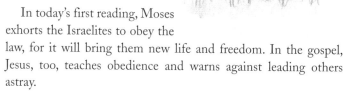

THE LAW OF LIFE

In today's first reading, Moses exhorts the Israelites to obey the law, for it will bring them new life and freedom. In the gospel, Jesus, too, teaches obedience and warns against leading others astray.

While we often associate law with restrictions and prohibitions, God's law is expansive and life-giving. Civil law is designed to protect society and its citizens; God's law frees us to love.

"For what other nation has a god so near to it as the LORD our God is whenever we call to him?" (Deut 4:7). *Lord, teach us to hear your word and to follow your ways.*

READINGS:
Deuteronomy 4:1, 5–9; Psalm 147; Matthew 5:17–19

Thursday, March 15

LISTENING

O that today you would listen to his voice! —Psalm 95:7

The last of the clinging oak leaves
    have given way to
    this year's buds;
And the tall, brown reeds
    bow backwards to
    the young green shoots.
Even the coats that protected
    the tender new buds have
    become litter underfoot.
There is no yearning
    for last year's
    blossoms;
They have borne their fruit
    and sustained us
    through winter's days.
Our hearts focus on today—
    its leaves and reeds,
    its blossoms and buds.
We place our hope
    in the life
    that springs forth....

READINGS:
Jeremiah 7:23–28; Psalm 95; Luke 11:14–23

Friday, March 16

BOUNDLESS CHARITY

"I will love them freely...."
　　　　　　　　—Hosea 14:4

What does it mean to love freely? Often our love for another is marked by self-centered reciprocity: You love me; I love you. You give to me; I give to you. Our charity can be measured or calculated without our realizing it.

God's love for us, however, is boundless and free. It is neither marked by reciprocity nor by calculation. What would our love look like if we let go of our measures? To give without looking for anything in return; to love without counting the cost; to share knowing we will never be an equal recipient.

Jesus calls us to love with all our heart, soul, mind, and strength. There are no bounds to God's love for us, or on Jesus' commandment of love.

Jesus, you love us freely. You feed us "...with the finest of the wheat and with honey from the rock" (Ps 81:16). Help us to be free from our measured ways so to love with boundless charity.

READINGS:
Hosea 14:2–10; Psalm 81; Mark 12:28–34

Saturday, March 17: Feast of Saint Patrick

BEGINNING AGAIN

"Your love is like a morning cloud,
like the dew that goes away early."
—Hosea 6:4

We are at the end of the third week of Lent. Ash Wednesday may seem like the image in today's reading from Hosea: an early hope that quickly vanished. There are key days and times when we make resolutions. January 1 and Ash Wednesday are two of them. How quickly, though, our grand plans dissolve, like the early dew!

"Let us know, let us press on to know the LORD; his appearing is as sure as the dawn" (Hos 6:3). Each day is a time to begin again, press on, try again. With God's help and grace all things are possible. So, as we approach the middle days of Lent, let us hope in the dawn and trust in God's strength in this journey to freedom and new life.

"Create in me a clean heart, O God, and put a new and right spirit within me" (Ps 51:10).

READINGS:
Hosea 6:1–6; Psalm 51; Luke 18:9–14

Fourth Sunday of Lent, March 18

LOVE BEYOND MEASURE

"Your brother has returned and your father has slaughtered the fattened calf because he has him back safe and sound."

—Luke 15:27

In the parable of the prodigal son, we find several interpretations of the word *home*. The younger son was not content in his father's house. The lure of the world and the "homes" that it offered were more than he could resist. He succumbed and, ironically, was left homeless! The older son seemed content in his father's house. He performed his duties and conformed to expectations. Yet this locked the home of his heart; his younger brother was left outside.

The father of these two brothers was aware that a true home exists in the depths of the soul. His was a home with open doors—*without conditions*—a home lighted by the love of God.

Loving God, you tell us that "those who seek the LORD lack for no good thing" (Ps 34:11). Grace us with your boundless love that our hearts and souls may be a warm and welcoming home for others.

READINGS:
Joshua 5:9, 10–12; Psalm 34; 2 Corinthians 5:17–21;
Luke 15:1–3, 11–32

Monday, March 19: Feast of Saint Joseph

SOUL NEWS

"Joseph, son of David, do not be afraid to take Mary as your wife into your home." —Matthew 1:20

There is no place for angels in our modern world. This technology-driven society has annexed our spiritual simplicity. How can we possibly understand something that we do not hear in our souls?

Disturbing news challenges us with shock. It can be too overwhelming, too much to absorb. We may even act as if we never heard it, and go on with our normal lives.

In Joseph, though, we have a model of how to respond to the challenges of our lives. Joseph was a true believer. He trusted and didn't count the cost of accepting God's will and desire for him. He was humble, allowing mystery to enter his heart.

Holy Joseph, "I will proclaim your faithfulness to all generations"
(Ps 89:1). May we nurture the person of Jesus in our lives as you did.
Bless us with your simplicity and charity. Give us the strength to
listen and to respond to God's challenges to us.

READINGS:
2 Samuel 7:4–5, 12–14, 16; Psalm 89; Romans 4:13, 16–18, 22;
Matthew 1:16, 18–21, 24

Tuesday, March 20

THE FAITH PERSPECTIVE

Jesus said to him, "Stand up, take your mat and walk."

—John 5:8

[But the Jews said], "It is not lawful for you to carry your mat."

—John 5:10

Perspective is everything! Jesus sees a blessing for the crippled man, a future. He wishes to make him well. The man sees himself cursed: "Sir, I have no one to put me in the pool" (John 5:7). And even though this man had suffered for thirty-eight years, the Jews were appalled that Jesus would do even God's work on the Sabbath.

In the experiences that God presents us with each day, do we see the blessing or the curse? Do we accept all happenings as coming from God? Do we sidestep the challenging ones? Do we bemoan the unpleasant? Can we see the blessing and grace?

Jesus, as we live through this day, give us your approach to life. May we bestow blessings while knowing that "the God of Jacob is our refuge" (Ps 46:1).

READINGS:
Ezekiel 47:1–9, 12; Psalm 46; John 5:1–3, 5–16

Wednesday, March 21

TIME APART

"My father is still working and I am also working."   —John 5:18

Whose work do I do? *What* work do I do? For *whom* do I work? Taking stock stops me in my tracks. I've found that it is so easy to get on the express train of workaholism, and not get off at any spiritual station. Even Jesus took time apart to be refueled by God's love. It is only this love that can truly restore my energy and adjust the lens through which I look at the world. Doing work for my own sake leads to a life of routine and comfort. Doing God's work opens me to a world of newness and awe.

Loving God, "every day I will bless you" (Ps 145:2) by remembering that I am employed by you and not myself. Feed me in the morning with your divine love that you may be satisfied by our work at the end of the day.

READINGS:
Isaiah 49:8–15; Psalm 145; John 5:17–30

Thursday, March 22

WATERS OF LIFE

"You search the scriptures because you think that in them you have eternal life…Yet you refuse to come to me to have life."

—John 5:39–40

I used to think that being totally recollected in prayer was enough for my salvation. Tapping into the love of God by reading the Bible caused flutters in my heart and soul. But then came the *knowledge* of Jesus! It is through *his* life that I have been given navigational tools for my own life. He has charted paths in my heart that cannot be found in any atlas. He has steered me from the safe coves of comfort into the deep ocean of risk. The compass of his love never wavers. His course for me changes every day. His desires for me are never static; they give my life the purpose and will to continue exploring the kingdom of God.

"Praise the LORD!…for his steadfast love endures forever"
(Ps 106:1). *O God, give me the grace to truly own your life within me so that I may be a carrier of the kingdom…wherever you take me.*

READINGS:
Exodus 32:7–14; Psalm 106; John 5:31–47

Friday, March 23

OPEN HEARTS

Then they tried to arrest
[Jesus]....Yet many in the crowd
believed in him. —John 7:30–31

How ironic that those with a
lifetime of learning turned their
backs on Jesus! Those with sharp
intellects and society's nod could not bow
to the possibilities of God.

Listening from the heart can be dangerous and risky business.
Yet childlike simplicity signals spiritual wisdom. It was the poor
with these attributes who truly captured the message of Jesus.
They opened their hearts and their homes to him and miracles
happened.

Jesus was truly at home with the marginalized, the sinner, tax
collectors, and lepers. He was moved by their open hearts, and
responded with boundless love. The Pharisees, who felt they had the
answers, had no room for this love. The good news that Jesus
brought challenged their way of life and inspired fear in their hearts.

Dear Jesus, I believe that "the LORD saves the crushed in spirit"
(Ps 34:18). Teach us to be poor in spirit so that no one and no thing
in this world means more than you.

READINGS:
Wisdom 2:1, 12–22; Psalm 34; John 7:1–2, 10, 25–30

Saturday, March 24

SPIRITUAL BALANCE

Then the Pharisees replied, "Surely you have not been deceived too, have you?"   —John 7:47

We live in a world of confusion. Late night movies have more appeal than early morning Mass. The stereo takes precedence over quiet moments spent with God. We have a desire for sushi more than for the Eucharist. Making it in this world takes all our energy. Have society's values usurped those of the family of God?

When our spiritual life is out of kilter, it seems all else is too. As Easter approaches, it is a good time to try to bring balance into our lives. Let the remaining days be ones of contemplation coupled with good works, so that we may not be deceived by the attractions of this life. May our only magnetic pull be toward doing God's will.

Jesus, "let the assembly of the peoples surround you" (Ps 7:8) as we once again embrace the reality and totality of your love. May we also embrace the challenge of loving you and release our selfishness and sin.

READINGS:
Jeremiah 11:18–20; Psalm 7; John 7:40–53

Fifth Sunday of Lent, March 25

STANDING BEFORE JESUS

Do not remember the former things....I am about to do a new thing.... —Isaiah 43:18–19

A woman is caught in the act of adultery. The Pharisees present her (and the law) to Jesus as a test. He responds, not with condemnation, but with a fresh insight. Sin may be the common ground of our human weakness, but its healing begins in full view before him.

Do I stand before Jesus to receive mercy, or do I slink away, still holding my sin inside?

I return to you today, Lord, with cries of joy, carrying the burdens of my sin. In your mercy you have done great things for me (Ps 126).

READINGS:
Isaiah 43:16–21; Psalm 126; Philippians 3:8–14; John 8:1–11

Monday, March 26: Solemnity of the Annunciation of the Lord

HERE I AM

"Greetings, favored one! The Lord is with you."　　　—Luke 1:28

Be gone fear, the Lord is near,
Raising the lowly on high.
In Mary, favored, the Lord has labored
To bring our salvation nigh!

Pondered perplexity finds direction
In promise of Spirit's coming
To a heart believing, and womb conceiving
The very child of God most loving.

So, be it also with me, fecundity,
Sufficient overshadowing to share.
In my life reign; in my deeds remain
Today, as Mary, be it Christ I bear.

"Here am I." Lord, open my ears in obedience this day, "I delight to do your will" (Ps 40:7–8).

READINGS:
Isaiah 7:10–14; Psalm 40; Hebrews 10:4–10; Luke 1:26–38

Tuesday, March 27

WHOSE AM I?

"…I do nothing on my own."
—John 8:28

Jesus was able to respond with compassion to each poor, sick, or sinful person who approached him for succor, as well as face the challenge of those whose hearts were closed to his word.

Where did he get his confidence and energy? He knew who was with—in fact, within—him. We, too, as children of the Father, have such an Eternal Source providing for all our needs.

Heedful God, hear my plea. "Do not hide your face from me in the day of my distress" (Ps 102:2). Reach down from the holy heights and let me know the touch of your presence in all I do today.

READINGS:
Numbers 21:4–9; Psalm 102; John 8:21–30

Wednesday, March 28

FREEDOM IN TRUTH

"…you will know the truth and the truth will make you free."
—John 8:32

Truth—reality as we perceive it from our own point of view—can be painful, embarrassing, convicting, alarming, overwhelming. No wonder we so often avoid it or deny it. Jesus invites us to see life and others from his own liberating vantage point, the truth that carries an eternal perspective. If we take some time today to listen to his word, its truth will transform our perceptions, and we will be set free.

"Blessed are you, O Lord," knower and sharer of the truth, "to be highly praised and highly exalted above all forever" (Dan 3:52). *Blessed are you in your freeing word, praiseworthy and glorious forever.*

READINGS:
Daniel 3:14–20, 52–56, 91–92, 95; John 8:31–42

Thursday, March 29

THE PROMISE

"As for you, you shall keep my covenant." —Genesis 17:9

"It's a keeper." After the sorting and selecting, the precious finds are worth holding onto. God promises offspring, land, kings, and nations to Abraham, who is only required to keep the covenant. Abraham was a "keeper" for God and kept the covenant.

Whom do I exclude from "keeper" status? Do I consider any person or group a "cast-off?" Do I recognize and rejoice that I, too, have been "kept" by God?

God our keeper, I recall your wondrous deeds, your signs, your words, your judgments (Ps 105:5). Today, I will rely on your keeping, you who remember your covenant forever!

READINGS:
Genesis 17:3–9; Psalm 105; John 8:51–59

Friday, March 30

WORDS MADE FLESH

"…even though you do not believe me, believe the works, so that you may know and understand that the Father is in me and I am in the Father."
—John 10:38

It has been said that actions speak louder than words, or that we should preach the good news always…and sometimes use words if necessary. Jesus spoke the truth *and* did good works. He did not limit himself to what was socially nor religiously acceptable in either sphere. And he faced the consequences: misunderstanding, threats of stoning and being hurled off cliffs, betrayal, denial, and even crucifixion. He knew the origin and purpose of his words and behavior.

Do I tell it like it is, walk the walk, and face the consequences of being a follower of Jesus?

"I love you, O LORD, my strength…" (Ps 18:1)*; rescue me from the clutches of my enemies. May you be praised in every word of my lips, in every step I take. Praised be the Lord!*

READINGS:
Jeremiah 20:10–13; Psalm 18; John 10:31–42

Saturday, March 31

PEACE IN ACTION

"I will make a covenant of peace with them...." —Ezekiel 37:26

Peace seems an elusive concept these days, as in former times. Wars continue in the interest of "peace, and saving lives." But there is no exchange rate when it comes to human life. Caiaphas proposed that Jesus die to avoid the destruction of their nation. Little did he know that God's plan was much bigger: the entire world has been granted salvation in the death and resurrection of Jesus, the Son of God.

Do I compromise with the Prince of Peace and consider some persons expendable in furthering some agenda in which we believe they have no place?

You are our guard, O Lord; you are our shepherd, we are your flock. You alone can redeem us from the hands of our conquerors, loosening our tongues and our feet for merriment and dancing. Turn our sorrow and mourning to joy and gladness (Jer 31:10–13).

READINGS:
Ezekiel 37:21–28; Jeremiah 31:10–13; John 11:45–57

Palm Sunday of the Lord's Passion, April 1

FAITHFUL LOVE

As we process and wave palms in honor of Jesus, we join the multitude rejoicing and praising God. Jesus was acclaimed by a delighted crowd ready to name him "King."

Yet, a little while later, we hear the Passion proclaimed and see this same Jesus betrayed and deserted. This crowd is neither rejoicing nor praising. They are intent on arresting Jesus as a criminal. Suffering and death await him, even denial by a chosen apostle. What a contrast!

In our own lives, too, there are moments of success and acclamation, pain and failure. Perhaps we have felt abandoned by those who were close to us.

Let us remember that we are not alone in the good times or in the bad. God is with us—the God whose love for us is faithful and unwavering. Resurrection always follows. Jesus has shown us the way.

O God, I trust in your love and faithfulness. Help me to deal with all the circumstances of my life.

READINGS:
Procession: Luke 19:28–40; Isaiah 50:4–7; Psalm 22;
Philippians 2:6–11; Luke 22:14—23:56

Monday of Holy Week, April 2

GOD'S VISION

Nothing is lost; it is just the cost of loving. Not one drop of blood, not one moment of suffering was empty of grace for Jesus. Neither is anything that *we do with love* ever wasted.

Jesus promised us abundant life. And we taste the fruits of that promise every now and then. That taste keeps us going and giving and loving in return.

On those days when fears and troubles fill our lives, let us remember that *every* experience holds grace—nothing is lost to our God.

"The LORD is my light and my salvation; whom shall I fear? The LORD is the stronghold of my life; of whom shall I be afraid?" (Ps 27:1).

READINGS:
Isaiah 42:1–7; Psalm 27; John 12:1–11

Tuesday of Holy Week, April 3

BROKEN YET BLESSED

Today we are called to live our brokenness under the blessing of God. Certainly, after all his protestations of faithfulness, Peter learned this lesson well.

Jesus invites us to wholeness. It is a lifetime journey. Along the way, we will meet our brokenness again and again. But brokenness is not a roadblock. It is a place to pause, sit quietly, and recognize our need for God. From there we set out a little wiser and a bit more grateful for God's mercy.

"In you, O LORD, I take refuge; let me never be put to shame. In your righteousness deliver me and rescue me; incline your ear to me and save me" (Ps 71:1–2).

READINGS:
Isaiah 49:1–6; Psalm 71; John 13:21–33, 36–38

Wednesday of Holy Week, April 4

CHOICE

The end is drawing near. The grain of wheat will fall to the ground. But in the case of Jesus, the grain of wheat falls willingly.

Jesus made a choice. His choice was twofold: to believe and to love. For Jesus, this would be followed to the heights of the transfiguration and to the depths of death on the cross.

Jesus chose to surrender to the will of God in his life. He was *not* powerless in the face of all that happened to him; on the contrary, he was committed and lived with his fears under the blessing of God. He believed and he loved to the end. Nothing would turn him away from his faithful love.

The experience of the cross does not make God's love for us any less. Jesus showed us that. The grain of wheat that is *all* of us will yield a rich harvest!

"It is zeal for your house that has consumed me" (Ps 69:9).

READINGS:
Isaiah 50:4–9; Psalm 69; Matthew 26:14–25

Holy Thursday, April 5

WAITING WITH HOPE

"You do not know now what I am doing, but later you will understand." —John 13:7

We look back on these forty days of Lent, feeling that we have been touched by grace, yet waiting on tomorrow for greater understanding.

Hindsight is a wonderful gift, not one to be regretted. It is learning from the past, for the good of our tomorrows. Jesus asks us to trust what we do not understand; to trust him, his presence, and his ways.

We may not understand what God is doing in our lives all the time but, like Peter, we are invited to trust that God desires our good. And that we are a meaningful and integral part of the kingdom that is taking shape.

"What shall I return to the LORD for all his [goodness] to me? I will lift up the cup of salvation and call on the name of the LORD" (Ps 116:12–13).

READINGS:
Exodus 12:1–8, 11–14; Psalm 116; 1 Corinthians 11:23–26; John 13:1–15

Good Friday, April 6

MEETING GRACE

Upon him was the punishment
that made us whole, and by his
bruises we are healed.

—Isaiah 53:5

Amazing, isn't it? The wounds of the
whip are the place of our healing. The suffering
and death of Jesus brought us wholeness and life. And it continues to do so. When we are empty, we can be filled; when we are poor, we can be enriched; when we surrender, we can be saved.

How does this happen? We go to the place of emptiness, poverty, and vulnerability and meet the grace that awaits us. Jesus walks with us, has gone before us, and is already there to touch and heal us. Will we have the courage to meet our grace as he did?

"Into your hand I commit my spirit; you have redeemed me,
O LORD, faithful God" (Ps 31:5).

READINGS:
Isaiah 52:13—53:12; Psalm 31; Hebrews 4:14–16, 5:7–9;
John 18:1—19:42

Holy Saturday, April 7

HOLY NIGHT

Holy light,
lead me through the darkness
   of this night
as you did our ancestors through the desert of old.
Holy light,
hallow the tomb of my flesh
and illumine my soul
that this night might shine as the day.
Holy light,
cast rays of grace into the chalice
of my sinfulness, filling it with shattering dawn.
Holy light,
shine with flame that freedom may laugh,
as tombs are open to the day of new life.

READINGS:
Genesis: 1:1—2:2; Exodus 14:15—15:1; Isaiah 55:1–11;
Psalm 42; Romans 6:3–11; Psalm 18; Luke 24:1–12

Easter Sunday, April 8

RESURRECTION SONG

Arise with me
through the days of all my hopes.
Arise with me
in the garden of my wildest dreams.
Arise with me
free of shackled limitations.
Arise with me
filled with grace of every dawn.
Arise with me
in the joy of life each morning.
Arise with me
into light of eternal day.
Arise with me.

READINGS:
Acts 10:34, 37–43; Psalm 118; Colossians 3:1–4; John 20:1–9

Contributors

SISTERS: Rosemary Campbell
Cecilia McManus
Regina Hudson
Ellen Farrell
Ellen Dauwer
Noreen Holly
Cheryl France
Edna Francis Hersinger
Anita Constance

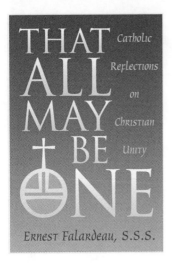

**That All
May Be One
*Catholic Reflections
on Christian Unity***

Ernest Falardeau, S.S.S.

Collects a year's worth of reflections from a Catholic perspective, sixty-four short essays on Christian unity as a spirituality that is nurtured by the Eucharist and celebrated throughout the liturgical seasons.

ISBN: 0-8091-3925-1 $14.95

*(Price and availability
subject to change)*

Ask at your local bookstore.

*For more information or to get a
free catalog of our publications, contact us at:*

Paulist Press · 997 Macarthur Boulevard · Mahwah, NJ 07430
1-800-218-1903 · Fax: 1-800-836-3161
E-mail: info@paulistpress.com
Visit our website at www.paulistpress.com

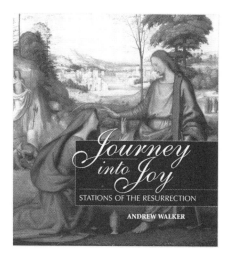

Biblical Meditations for Lent

Carroll Stuhlmueller, C.P.

Readings for each weekday as well as the Sundays of each of the three cycles are summarized, and reflections for each day are given based on scriptural scholarship.

ISBN: 0-8091-2089-5   Price $9.95

*(Price and availability
subject to change)*

Ask at your local bookstore.

*For more information or to get a
free catalog of our publications, contact us at:*

Paulist Press · 997 Macarthur Boulevard · Mahwah, NJ 07430
1-800-218-1903 · Fax: 1-800-836-3161
E-mail: info@paulistpress.com
Visit our website at www.paulistpress.com

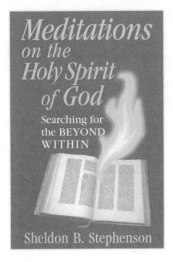

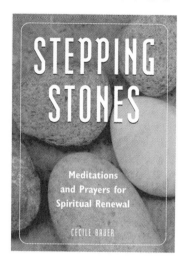

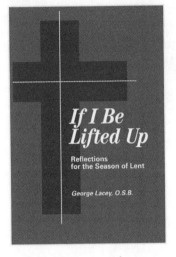

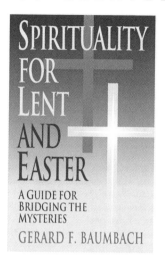

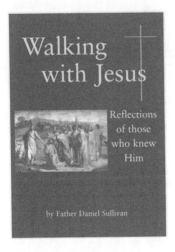

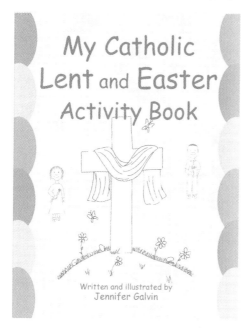

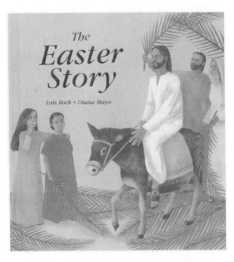

ADVANCE RESERVATION FORM

Living the Days of Lent 2008

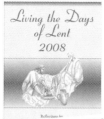

Makes a Great Gift!

Pages contributed by the Sisters of Charity of Saint Elizabeth; edited by Anita M. Constance, S.C.

Paulist's best selling series of daily Lenten devotions uses scripture, prose reflections, and original prayers and poems to center readers' minds and souls and gently bring them to readiness for Easter. With these daily meditations, readers learn to open themselves to the risks and rewards of living a fuller life, of finding compassion from themselves and others, and of resting more deeply in God's loving care.

Living the Days of Lent 2008—
- runs daily from Ash Wednesday through Easter Sunday.
- ends each day's selection with the daily lectionary citations.
- includes pointed challenges for one's thoughts and actions.
- comes in a tear-out, page-a-day format for handy use.

-------------------------------- *Reserve Your Copy Today!* --------------------------------

Please send me _____ copy(ies) of: **Living the Days of Lent 2008 #0-8091-4461-7 @ $4.95 ea.**

Please include applicable sales tax, and postage and handling ($3.50 for first $20 plus 50¢ for each additional $10 ordered)—check or money order only payable to **Paulist Press**.

Enclosed is my check or money order in the amount of $ _____

Name _____

Position _____

Institution _____

Street _____

City/State/Zip _____

Phone # _____

For more information or to receive a free catalog of our publications, contact us at:

Paulist Press™ 997 Macarthur Blvd., Mahwah, N.J. 07430 • 1-800-218-1903
FAX 1-800-836-3161 • E-MAIL: info@paulistpress.com • www.paulistpress.com